Employee Performance Evaluation Examples

+ Tips for Streamlining the Writing Process

Lewis Crestwell

© 2021

Inside this resource:

- Evaluations (still) matter
- Make evaluations nothing more than a formality
- Don't throw the whole employee away
- Streamline the process
- Informal check-ins
- Employee self-evaluation
- What to include in a written evaluation
- What to avoid
- Take note of oddities
- Give feedback
- Powerful descriptors
- **Full-length sample evaluation narratives**
  - *GENERAL EXAMPLE*
  - *ADMINISTRATIVE ROLE*
  - *TECHNICAL ROLE*
  - *CREATIVE ROLE*
  - *PATIENT CARE ROLE*
  - *EDUCATOR/TRAINER ROLE*
  - *SALES ROLE*
  - *MANAGERIAL ROLE*
- Special Circumstances
- Presenting the Evaluation

Evaluations [still] matter.

The entire process of formal evaluations is tedious and time-consuming. So why bother with them at all?

In addition to the fact that many corporations want a formal record of employee performance, American workers aged 18-34 report that they believe formal feedback from superiors is important*. However, the same demographic of employees also think that the traditional process of annual reviews is less than ideal*.

Is there a way, then, to satisfy the admittedly archaic human resource requirements at many organizations and provide employees with feedback they desire that also serves as a formal evaluation of their performance? When asked, workers reported that more frequent but less formal check-ins with their managers and a more open line of communication could the solution*.

Evaluating employees in a more casual manner on a more regular basis can be helpful for you, too. Reviewing performance in small snippets throughout the year and conversing casually with employees helps them identify areas to improve upon more quickly than waiting for formal evaluations, and builds a better working relationship that will help you make evaluations faster and more streamlined.

And, when it's time for formal written evaluations, refer to the examples given towards the back of this resource to make your process as quick and efficient as possible.

*Hernandez, Rob. 2015. Retrieved from https://www.fastcompany.com/3052988/heres-what-millennials-want-from-their-performance-reviews.

Make annual evaluations nothing more than a formality.

If you follow steps to evaluate snippets of an employee's performance throughout the year, the formal process of written evaluations and one-on-one reviews becomes nothing more than that: *a formality*. If employees know what they're doing well throughout the quarter or year, and can further improve upon their strengths at the same time that they have a chance to work on their weaknesses, formal evaluations can be nothing more than a follow-up on conversations you've already had throughout the evaluation period in lower stress settings. Doing so reduces stress not only on you, but also on your employees.

The feedback given in the formal evaluation of the employee, in most cases, should not be a surprise. If there are concerns about substandard performance throughout the evaluation period, they should be addressed in a far timelier manner than waiting for annual evaluations to roll around. For employees who exceed expectations, their achievements should not go unacknowledged until they receive the formal evaluation.

Certainly, the process of writing formal evaluation narratives is non-negotiable in many organizations. That's okay. Later in this book, I lay out **sixteen complete evaluation narratives**, including how I phrase evaluations for employees who excel and also those with more room to improve in eight separate areas of concentration. With an infinite and ever-changing list of tasks on your desk, don't spend more time writing evaluations than you spend managing. Feel free to tailor my examples to your employees and use as much or as little of each of sample as you choose.

Don't throw the whole employee away.

When writing your evaluations, even the ones for the employees failing to meet standards, remember this: *Do not throw that employee away.*

I speak this mantra as a professional who has worked in many facets from the very lowest entry-level position on up through the corporate structure as I slowly earned one, two, then three degrees and, even more slowly, transformed both the way I present myself and the quality of my work overall. I've had excellent managers, but, even more often, I've had poor managers who failed completely at inspiring me and lifting me up. I've had good evaluations and bad. I've worked with colleagues who are exceptional, and others that I'd rather never work alongside again. I personally know how it feels to receive evaluations on both ends of the spectrum, and I've had hardworking colleagues vent to me when they receive a negative evaluation seemingly at the whim of the manager that day.

Chances are, you've experienced the same range of emotions. Few professionals who have risen to the rank of manager have gone their entire working life without receiving criticism. Do you recall how you felt when a superior described something negative about your performance? Did you feel embarrassed, inspired to change, or perhaps angry that your positive attributes were going unnoticed? Did the phrasing and delivery of the constructive feedback affect your perception of the comments?

Reflect for a moment about how you receive constructive feedback and what you do with it. Does it always feel good to know you have room for improvement? Has it been helpful or hurtful in the past to hear that you have performed poorly or failed to meet a goal? If you received an evaluation that was nothing but negativity and examples of what you did poorly, would you be inspired to do better, or would you feel more inclined to check out and stop trying to impress someone who obviously doesn't recognize your positive qualities?

People are the core of every business. Every industry needs people. You need your people. You need your people to work hard, and you need your people to feel inspired to deliver what you, the manager, need from them.

Certainly, you're a "people" yourself. Human beings are subject to emotions, personal preferences, and opinions. As someone responsible for managing and evaluating other employees, your human nature has a strong likelihood of influencing how you feel about your subordinates. It's not wrong to have strong feelings and personal opinions. However, it's not helpful to clutter your formal evaluation with personal opinions and bias. You have full control over what you write about those employees. It is imperative that the subjective thoughts about your employees are kept at bay and are not a part of formal evaluations.

Written evaluations should be objective in nature. To help accomplish this, the specific examples you give in your evaluations should be quantitative or, if qualitative, should be concrete and specific. Refer to actual numbers and statistics whenever possible. Cite specific examples about incidents that occurred. List the names of certifications or training received whenever possible. Avoid referring to work broadly and subjectively as "good" or "bad," even though all humans surely have traits that are, generally speaking, good or bad.

When you find yourself evaluating an employee whose "bad"

traits tend to stand out a little more than the good ones, take a deep breath and remind yourself to not throw the whole employee away. Keep your written evaluation professional and devoid of personal opinion. Remember that none of your employees are perfect, and that you need these people to meet the goals of organization. Recall that a few missteps, errors, or shortcomings doesn't mean someone is not the right fit for your team. Rather, it may mean they need more guidance, another chance, stronger feedback, or additional training. Even if there's an overwhelmingly negative component of an employee's performance, **don't just throw the whole employee away.**

Acknowledge the good. Inspire your employees to continue striving for improvement. Be honest but professional about the behaviors and elements that need to change. Be clear about how the employee's habits could change to result in a better evaluation in the future. Be mindful about the impact reading an evaluation has on an employee. Take opportunities to build your employees up. But, whatever you do, don't throw the whole employee away.

Streamline the Process

How?

- Offer informal monthly check-ins with employees
- Keep running log of achievements that parallels the job description
    - Encourage them to do the same to streamline their self-evaluation process
- Don't blindside employees with negative feedback or areas that need improvement during formal evaluations, but address these areas throughout the year

If your employee takes responsibility for part of their evaluation, you won't be required to have the memory of an elephant to recall all of the projects on which he or she has worked, nor the outcomes of those projects and whether goals were met.

Having served in a wide variety of professional roles myself, both as an employee and a supervisory position, I have tried out multiple strategies for keeping track of my own improvements to ensure that due credit is not missed. The best way I have found is to keep my own running self-evaluation that I can add data to regularly.

Collect verbal feedback during informal weekly or monthly check-ins over coffee. Encourage your employees to jot down their accomplishments for the week in a document on their computers or in a notepad. You also could keep a running list on your computer or in a notebook and make quick notes during the check-ins about each employee, if your number of subordinates is small enough to facilitate keeping notes on each one.

When specific issues or opportunities arise, offer the constructive feedback on the spot rather than waiting for a formal review process to do so.

Informal Check-ins

Why?

Checking in routinely with your staff will make it second nature to reflect on their accomplishments or areas that need improvement.

During regular, informal check-ins, even in a group setting, you will get to know each employee on a more personal level, which will help streamline the process of writing formal evaluations when the time comes.

If there are areas that would benefit from improvement, it is less intimidating to the employee to bring up suggestions in a routine, low-stress check-in than to arrange a special meeting to discuss shortcomings. No one likes hearing the boss unexpectedly say, "I need to see you in my office."

How?

Use any format that fits easily into your weekly routine and feels comfortable and natural for you and your employees.

One-on-one

- Schedule informal sit-downs with each employee on a monthly basis
- The casual environment encourages engagement
- Check-ins can be done over coffee, lunch, or snacks

Small group check-ins

- Likely not appropriate/effective for every employee
- Can motivate employees by hearing their colleague's accomplishments
- Can also dissuade employees from engaging with you, the superior, if louder colleagues dominate the conversation or they are fearful of bringing up some points in the group setting
- Decreases the amount of time spent on check-ins since multiple employees can be engaged at once

Employee Self Evaluation

Why?

If your corporation does not explicitly require that the employees perform their own write-up for submission, there's no need to mandate a formal document.

However, what can be helpful for you as you conduct your reviewss is a short summary or list of accomplishments submitted to you by employees for reference.

The easiest way to ensure the employees keep up with their self-evaluations is to have them start a very simple document at the beginning of the evaluation period or upon hire.

How?

Consider formatting a simple document listing the ten most important factors that you will evaluate and ask the employee to write one or sentences under each of the ten items when a relevant event occurs or on a weekly or monthly basis.

Send a message or make an announcement at certain times, such as Friday afternoons at 1:00, that employees should consider spending about 120 seconds reflecting on the accomplishments for the week.

You also could customize a more in-depth self-evaluation document using the job descriptions for each employee's position:

Creating a template for employee self-evaluations:

1. Summarize each main point of the job description in one or two blurbs.
2. Paste into a document with room beside or below each point for the employee to add information.
3. Remind employees on a weekly basis to add data, list achievements, or journal accomplishments in the appropriate section of the document.
4. Once the document is set up, the weekly self-reflections can take as little as 120 seconds to jot reminders.

Gather additional feedback from the team:

Ask for feedback from other teammates that showcase their peers' willingness to strive for team excellence. A great way to collect these blurbs is to organize a central collection point for your employees to jot down a line or two about a team member who went out of their way to help out. You could have a basket with blank notecards nearby, or something more formal, such as my *Thank You* logbook that sits nicely on a desk or table to collect shout-outs that employees can flip through as they please:

(Available on Amazon).

What to include in a written evaluation

- Time frame that the evaluation covers
  - *"During the past year…"*
  - *"During the past quarter…"*
  - *"For the time period of March 2021 to June 2021…"*
- Feedback specific to all aspects of the employee's job description, not just a select few
- Positive feedback
  - *"Employee excelled at strict time management and met one hundred percent of deadlines for projects this quarter."*
- Constructive feedback referencing areas for improvement *with recommendations for how to improve upon them*
  - *"Employee may consider obtaining a certification in organizational leadership to improve upon communication skills with subordinates."*
- *For applicable employees,* the job description for the next tier of responsibility and/or the recommendation for a promotion or raise

What to avoid

- Avoid describing a negative feedback as "always" or "never"
  - Is the employee truly "always" in a bad mood?
  - Does the employee truly "never" meet a deadline?
- Avoid stating "in my opinion."
  - The evaluation should truly not be opinion
  - Objectives should either be clearly met or clearly missed
  - Achievements should be quantifiable and describable by name
- Avoid evaluating an employee's *personality* rather than *workplace performance*
  - It may be annoying that Wanda makes small talk every single time she passes you in the hallway, but does it make her bad at her job?

Take note of oddities

The Curious Case of the (-)(+) [Negative Positives]:

Avoid citing these qualities that may *appear* positive but are not always positive attributes. For example, it may be nice that an employee never takes vacation days because you don't have to find coverage for that position, but it could be a sign of a toxic work environment to reward an employee for doing so.

- Working regular overtime
- Not taking vacations
- Not calling in sick when actually sick
- Working through lunch breaks
- Over-delegating tasks

The Curious Case of the (+)(-) [Positive Negatives]:

These are positive qualities that may seem like negatives at first glance but could actually reflect strengths of employees.

- Notifying management of an error
- Taking a sabbatical
- Asking for more training
- Communicating to superior a feeling of overwhelm related to burden of tasks and responsibilities

Give Feedback

How to phrase criticism constructively:

- Give concrete examples
- Paint a picture of what an ideal outcome may be
- Ensure that praise is given where applicable and that the entire employee evaluation is not comprised solely of constructive criticism
- When possible, envelop a sentence detailing the need for improvement between two positives
- Refer to the criticism as constructive "advice" rather than criticism to create a more positive connotation
- Remember that each employee has value in his or her own way and that most people want to perform well

Powerful Descriptors

Examples for starting sentences in written evaluations.

For above average performance:

- Excels at…
- Exceeds the standard goal of…
- Top XX% of his/her peers…
- Master of…
- Proficient at…
- Showed talent in…
- Experienced with…
- Optimal levels of achievement as shown by…
- Increased productivity by…
- Continually assesses and seeks improvement by…
- Develops successful strategies such as…
- Empowers colleagues by…

Average performance:

- Met the standard…
- Showed improvement…
- Did a good job at…
- Beginning to master…
- Showed some growth in…

Below average/needs improvement:

- Could consider improving by…
- May benefit from additional education/training to…
- Fell somewhat short of the goal by…
- In the future, may consider a change in habits to…

A single employee may receive feedback on the evaluation that includes some above average performance, average performance, and below average performance depending on the criteria being measured. Generally, an employee is not completely perfect nor completely incompetent. The challenge in writing evaluations is to properly balance the feedback between praising the success of the employee and offering constructive advice to further challenge and help the employee direct his or her energy towards improvement.

SAMPLE
EVALUATION
NARRATIVES

GENERAL EXAMPLE

Sample factors to evaluate:

- Communication
- Collaboration and teamwork
- Interpersonal skills
- Ability to solve problems
- Accuracy or quality of work
- Attendance
- Ability to meet deadlines
- Time management
- Creative solutions/innovation
- Ability to adapt
- Taking personal responsibility/accountability for outcomes
- Improvement from previous goals or previous evaluation periods

[General Example]
Excellent Performance

Over the past year, Desmond has worked as a Technical Assistant and demonstrated superb work ethic and the impressive ability to meet 100% of his professional goals in the workplace. Through his involvement within the team process improvement projects last quarter, Desmond demonstrated impressive leadership skills by taking charge of the weekly meetings, delegating the task of keeping careful records of the meetings to an appropriate layperson, and showcasing unparalleled communication skills by keeping team members who were not serving on the committee informed of the developments and direction of the process improvement project. The results of this process improvement project included an increase in productivity and team morale. Further, during peer evaluations this quarter, Desmond received top ratings from his colleagues, who unanimously indicated that he is an invaluable member of the team who brings a positive attitude and top-notch organization skills to every project. Further yet, functioning far above his designated duties, Desmond voluntarily chose to attend a certification class to further advance his education and obtained a Leadership certificate which will continue to help Desmond serve his team in the future. Desmond has demonstrated workplace capabilities that exceed those necessary for his current position, and with the understanding that Desmond is seeking a promotion to a Tier II Technician, it is my recommendation that Desmond receives this promotion and correlating salary increase of 10% effective immediately.

[General Example]
Poor Performance with Room for Improvement

Issues Addressed:

- ❏ Tardiness/absenteeism
- ❏ Difficulty focusing on task at hand
- ❏ Time wasted socializing with peers

During this evaluation period, Li served in the role of Technical Assistant. Li has worked in this capacity for two years at the time of this evaluation. Li has a friendly and outgoing demeanor at work, which makes her approachable for other team members who have questions or need guidance in their own positions. Li's time may be better leveraged if personal conversations unrelated to work were kept to a minimum. When Li is able to focus, she is a creative, outside-the-box thinker with enthusiasm for new ideas. Li's energy and problem-solving ability may result in even greater productivity if Li arrived to work at her scheduled time on a more regular basis. If Li improved upon the aforementioned criteria, Li could find herself ranked in the top fifty percent of employees. During this evaluation period, Li is rated in the top ninety percent of employees.

ADMINISTRATIVE ROLE

Sample administrative tasks to evaluate:

- Provides administrative support to the office
- Receives incoming telephone calls, emails, faxes, and visitors
- Utilizing a word processor to support the development of presentations, documents, spreadsheets, or other paper forms of data
- Organizing, filing, and maintaining documents

[Administrative Role]
Excellent Performance

During the past year, Reginald has demonstrated an incredible commitment to meeting and exceeding the standards set forth in his job description. As an administrator, Reginald is a vital member of our team. Many of the inner workings of the company rely heavily upon Reginald completing his work in a timely and effective manner. The standard for his position dictates that Reginald should be present and available at or near the reception desk to help clients both internally and externally with communication. Reginald demonstrated commitment to the quality of his work by not only maintaining an open and friendly demeanor at the reception area, but also engaging clients in meaningful conversation while they awaited their scheduled meeting times. On more than one occasion, clients referred to Reginald by name and remarked that his friendly smile and banter made them feel welcome and excited to partner with the company. Further, Reginald answered telephone calls and emails in a timely manner, rarely leaving clients on hold for extended amount of time, and offering an apology, explanation, and frequent check-ins when circumstances outside his control mandated that a client's telephone call be left on hold for a period of time. Reginald demonstrated incredible organization skills with both paper and electronic documents, and assisted internal staff in locating the correct forms when needed. Overall, Reginald has demonstrated his value as an administrator, and due to the services he has provided the company over the past year, I am recommending that Reginald receive a ten percent raise in salary.

[Administrative Role]
Poor Performance with Room for Improvement

Issues Addressed:

❏ Unfriendly demeanor that is unwelcoming to clients
❏ Abandoning the front desk and failing to be present to assist clients

During this evaluation period, Nora assisted our unit by working in an administrative capacity. Nora is responsible to maintain a physical presence at the desk to greet and direct clients, receive phone calls, and maintain organization of paper documents in the filing cabinets in the front office. Nora is punctual and only arrived to work late a few times this year. This year, Nora took over responsibility of operating the fax machine in the office and spent part of her day nearly every day delivering documents to other offices. While it is important to keep the fax machine area clear and organized, Nora may be better able to serve and direct clients if she was available at the front desk for a larger portion of the day. Nora has a vast knowledge of the contacts within the building and usually knows where to direct clients when they arrive. However, Nora may be able to help clients feel more welcome if she greeted people who approach the desk rather than turning away. Nora has a wonderful sense of humor and has a working relationship with several other offices within our building.

TECHNICAL ROLE

Sample technical tasks to evaluate:

- Identify repairs needed and performing necessary repairs
- Assist in the setup of physical processes and equipment
- Maintain a safe work area free from hazards or identifies safety hazards

[Technical Role]
Excellent Performance

Katie has been with our company for nine months out of the past twelve-month evaluation period, and as a new employee, Katie has proven herself to be a skilled technician and a reliable team member. Katie completed the orientation to her new role in six weeks' time, demonstrating a strong work ethic and the ability to work autonomously. When Katie had questions, she did not hesitate to ask her superiors to ensure that she completed quality work. Katie has continuously improved upon her skill set, and independently completed her certification program six months into her new position. Katie inspires other team members with her positivity and willingness to track down the right answer. Over the next evaluation period, Katie's goals are to work on her second tier of certification and mentor new employees. If Katie reaches both of these goals, she should be promoted to Technician II following the next evaluation period.

[Technical Role]
Poor Performance with Room for Improvement

Issues addressed:

- ❏ Difficulty staying on task
- ❏ Failure to complete necessary certifications to perform job
- ❏ Low productivity
- ❏ Lack of initiative within assigned role

Lupe has been performing preventative maintenance on our machines for the past twelve months. He joined our company while completing his certification process through a local trades school. Lupe has an inquisitive mind and often asks questions to ensure that he knows what work needs to be done. Lupe is helpful with extra duties around the shop, such as sweeping and washing windows even when those duties are not assigned to him. Lupe's talents, however, may be better utilized by working exclusively within his assigned role. Lupe completed preventative maintenance on approximately half of the machines assigned to him for maintenance. Lupe may benefit from additional training in time management during the next evaluation period to ensure that one hundred percent of machines are maintained. For the upcoming evaluation period, our in-house trainer will be working with Lupe to apply his talents towards performing assigned maintenance on necessary machines. It would also be beneficial for Lupe to resume his classes at the trades school and continue pursuing his certification pertinent to his current position. Lupe is bright and talented and is a valued member of our team.

CREATIVE ROLE

Sample creative tasks to evaluate:

- Develop novel ideas that have potential applications across an organization
- Stay up-to-date with ever-changing trends and styles
- Inspire other designers and/or creative team members
- Communicate with clients, creative team, or other teams across an organization
- Work on appropriate tasks and meet deadlines

[Creative Role]
Excellent Performance

Jerome embraced the next level of inspiration with his creative work over the past year. He showed up on time with fresh ideas and confidently pitched new concepts to his team members, welcoming constructive feedback. Jerome performed regular assessments of the market to ensure that he was familiar with the most recent trending fashions and styles to best resonate with our customer base. Jerome's positive and inclusive attitude inspired the entire team and validated new and fresh ideas and perspectives that colleagues brought forth. Jerome demonstrated polite and considerate communication among his team and also during calls with clients and was never afraid to ask direct questions to ensure that the team was all on the same page. Through Jerome's tireless work and dedication to the mission, one hundred percent of relevant deadlines were met and Jerome's team followed up on pertinent client communication in a timely manner. Jerome demonstrated a dedication to working on the most important tasks at appropriate times and his energy helped ensure that team members also stayed on task and met deadlines.

[Creative Role]
Poor Performance with Room for Improvement

Issues addressed:

- ❑ Difficulty receiving constructive feedback
- ❑ Does not work well within assigned team
- ❑ Failure to meet necessary deadlines

Guin is an experienced graphic artist who joined our team at the beginning of the past evaluation period. Guin has an impressive portfolio and has a unique perspective on graphic design which is evident in the projects that Guin has submitted. Guin's creativity and talents may be better appreciated and our clients would be better served if her projects were completed prior to or on the respective deadline. Guin is a member of an equally talented team of graphic artists who appreciate the skills and visions that Guin brings to the table. It may better benefit the team if Guin exercised more open communication and listened to their feedback with respect to their unique ideas. Guin is a valuable member of our team and has potential to excel in her position.

PATIENT CARE ROLE

Sample patient care tasks to evaluate:

- Execute physician's plan of care for patients with patient safety in mind
- Demonstrate clinical expertise when reviewing medication and care orders
- Triage patient care, unexpected changes in patient status, and staffing considerations
- Exhibit proper handling of biological samples
- Prioritize patient safety

[Patient Care Role]
Excellent Performance

This quarter, Mel exemplified the qualities of a fully successful nurse while working on our ward. She showed up on time, fully prepared to take report from the previous shift. Mel's approachable demeanor made it easy for nurses to give reports on patients to her. Her positive attitude is the reason that Mel was chosen to precept a new employee this quarter, and also oriented a nursing student to our ward for one shift. Mel has impeccable attention to detail, resulting in zero medication errors. Mel's attention to detail when reviewing orders helped her discover two separate mistakes that physicians made when writing orders, which Mel followed up on appropriately and was able to correct, ensuring the safety of our patients. While our ward received an unprecedented influx of patients admitted, Mel appropriately triaged patient care, accepting care of more patients per shift than in prior quarters due to staffing obstacles within our facility, and exemplified a positive attitude while continuing to advocate for patient safety. Mel served on the nursing council and helped develop a project to increase the morale of our staff, resulting in a unit-wide gift exchange which received positive feedback from staff. During the next quarter, Mel has a goal of obtaining an advanced patient intervention certification to better serve her patients.

[Patient Care Role]
Poor Performance with Room for Improvement

Issues addressed:

- ❏ Substance misuse/abuse
- ❏ Absenteeism
- ❏ Patient care complaints

Francis is a licensed practical nurse on our patient care team. Francis has a wealth of experience spanning almost ten years in the rehabilitation sector of health care. When Francis is at work, his peers describe him as helpful and jovial. Francis could be even more helpful if he arrived on time to each of his scheduled shifts. Francis has a desire to improve and continue learning. After a positive urine screen for illicit substances, Francis willingly began working with our substance abuse team, who has reported excellent communication from Francis and no further positive urine screens for illicit substances. Francis has a very direct approach with his patients. His bedside manner is not always well received by our entire patient population. Francis may be better able to serve a more diverse population if he remains more neutral at the bedside when caring for patients. Overall, Francis met the minimum standards of care for our position and has the potential to exceed the standards of care with more punctual attendance and continued adherence to the substance misuse protocol.

EDUCATOR/TRAINER ROLE

Sample educator tasks to evaluate:

- Design, implement, and evaluate training programs/regimens
- Lead seminars, workshops, classes, and/or lectures designed to educate & instruct
- Prepare effective education materials such as brochures, videos, handouts, and equipment
- Provides adequate support and mentorship for new employees

[Educator/Trainer Role]
Excellent Performance

This year has been the third year that Flint has served as our corporate educator. In his role, Flint is responsible for maintaining and adjusting the training regimens for newly hired employees as needed as well as managing the mentorship program for current employees learning new skills or needing to improve upon existing skills. Included in these responsibilities is the need to edit and maintain slides to be presented at new hire orientation as well as generating the paper handouts for the orientees. As the manager of the mentorship program, Flint was responsible for identifying highly skilled employees to serve as mentors as well as fostering individual learning opportunities for mentees requiring extra attention. Flint far exceeded his described responsibilities by identifying opportunities to improve the mentorship program. He developed a survey for all employees to take to help identify special skills and talents as well as the desire to teach and serve as a mentor. Through these surveys, Flint identified twelve additional mentors to help teach new employees. As a result of the transformation of the mentorship program, new employees reported greater job satisfaction than the employees who began working during the year prior. Flint has set a goal to further expand the mentorship program to new departments next year and to develop a unique certification project for mentors to work towards.

[Educator/Trainer Role]
Poor Performance with Room for Improvement

Issues addressed:

- ❏ Performance and abilities not consistent with what were demonstrated during the interview process
- ❏ Appearing to be overwhelmed by a new role to the point of inaction

Sydney is in charge of the special education division of our institution. Sydney is new in this role during this evaluation period, and brings five years of relevant experience to this position. Overseeing a classroom of nineteen children excelling in their academic studies and requiring more challenging coursework is a unique task for which Sydney demonstrated potential to excel during her interview period. The mission to fulfill the unique needs of our individual students would be best met if the strategies proposed during the initial interview and probation period of Sydney's tenure are brought to fruition. The role of special education is certainly a challenging one. Sydney's ambition and innovative ideas are the reason she is a good fit for our team. Just as colleagues rely on Sydney's teamwork to facilitate completing their own workload, Sydney may find support in brainstorming with her teammates and working together to best meet the common goal. Sydney's hard work and capability will be helpful tools over the next evaluation period in striving to meet her expectations.

SALES ROLE

Sample sales tasks to evaluate:

- Communicate effectively with customers/clients to assist them in meeting their needs
- Be knowledgeable and familiar with products and/or services as applicable
- Identify opportunities to upsell
- Meet established quotas

[Sales Role]
Excellent Performance

Ki is a valuable salesperson on our team. Over the past quarter, Ki has taken the initiative to vastly improve her knowledge and familiarity with the products, resulting in an increase in sales. Compared to the previous quarter, Ki increased the number of products sold by 13 percent, which produced a 27 percent increase in revenue generated. Ki's quarterly commission bonus reflects our appreciation of her hard work and skill at connecting with prospective and existing customers. Ki has maintained critical relationships with our highly valued customers, and routinely receives positive feedback referencing her by name. In her downtime this quarter, Ki also independently organized and started a process improvement project to better store available merchandise for ease of locating specific products requested by customers. Ki's dedication to the team in generating critical sales and her ability to close deals with a variety of customers landed Ki in the top five percent of salespeople in the company this quarter.

[Sales Role]
Poor Performance with Room for Improvement

Issues addressed:

- ❑ Spending time on personal phone
- ❑ Vocalizing personal opinions that do not serve customers
- ❑ Decreased sales metrics
- ❑ Need to work under a mentor after failing to meet goals independently

Auggie is a team member on the sales floor of our downtown location. This quarter, Auggie made contact with a variety of prospective and established customers. The company-wide goal for salespeople is to assist customers in identifying their individual needs and then locate the appropriate product to satisfy those needs. Auggie may be better equipped to reach this goal if his personal and unique opinions were kept to a minimum when conversing with customers. Auggie has the ability to speak fluently with customers which carries with it the potential to be an excellent salesperson. If Auggie engaged with customers with the same regularity that he engages with personal calls and texts on his phone, he may find more opportunities to close sales transactions, which would positively affect his returns. This quarter, Auggie's sales were better than three percent of the company. His gross sales fell by forty-seven percent compared to last quarter. Next quarter, Auggie will have the opportunity to learn from a mentor at our site and the chance to improve his sales numbers.

MANAGERIAL ROLE

Sample management tasks to evaluate:

- Ensures that the department meets its objectives by effectively leading employees
- Maintains staff by encouraging positive morale through engagement and recruiting new employees when applicable
- Ensures that the work environment is safe and conducive to work
- Upholds legal standards in the office
- Manages and encourages professional growth among team

[Manager Role]
Excellent Performance

During this evaluation period, Brandon has demonstrated his outstanding value to our organization through his extraordinary leadership of a team of 22 subordinates. Brandon performed beyond expectations as set forth in his written job description by increasing the productivity of the team that he manages by 27% during the past year, exhibiting an increase in each quarter for four consecutive quarters. Brandon onboarded two new staff members who, under his guidance, integrated with the team and quickly came up to speed to further advance the mission of our organization. Brandon organized and hosted monthly staff meetings, compiling the most recent sales data and performing statistical analyses of each data point for presentation to an audience of 20-30 individuals per meeting. Brandon's employees reported positive job satisfaction working under his guidance.

[Manager Role]
Poor Performance with Room for Improvement

Issues addressed:

- ❑ New to managerial role and requiring more education
- ❑ Unwillingness to confront employees with substandard performance
- ❑ Hands-off management approach not conducive to producing positive results

Erin is a new manager over this division. In Erin's time in management thus far, Erin has demonstrated a positive demeanor that facilitated working relationships with many members of the team. Erin's training in her role as a manager is ongoing and will include strategies to initiate and follow up on conversations and formal meetings with employees who are not meeting the acceptable standards of their position, after which time the goal is for Erin to feel more comfortable and confident initiating and directing these employee encounters independently. Fifteen percent of Erin's subordinates failed to perform satisfactorily in their individual roles this quarter, which is approximately fifty percent higher than the average rate of unsatisfactory performance among subordinates managed by Erin's colleagues. Additional training combined with Erin's strong work ethic should result in improved results during the following evaluation period. Erin is punctual and organized, qualities that lend themselves well to positive outcomes in a management position.

Special Circumstances

New Employee

Marie joined our team six months ago at the midway point of our evaluation period. In the time that she has been here...

Monte is new in this position. During his orientation period, he demonstrated a strong work ethic and ability to learn independently and began to establish working relationships within the team...

Employee with Extended Leave During Evaluation Period

Rachel has been with our company for three years. During the past annual evaluation period, Rachel worked on-site for approximately six months, worked exclusively from home for one month, and took five months of approved FMLA time away from her position. Despite having been actively engaged for just seven of the past twelve months, Rachel still pursued the goals she had set for herself and through her dedication and impressive time management, was able to achieve the majority of them by...

Presenting the Evaluation

In most companies, the written evaluation is presented to the employee as part of a verbal review.

Sample Overview of Verbal Review

- Major topics in the evaluation should not come as a surprise
    - If you utilize the regular check-ins aforementioned, you will have ample opportunities to bring up pertinent feedback before the formal evaluation.
    - If you are feeling anxious or hesitant about the one-on-one meeting with a staff member, ask yourself if it's because some of the feedback you are preparing to share will be new to the employee:

- For habitually substandard employees, a paperwork trail should be started when appropriate rather than waiting for the formal evaluation.
- Human Resources should be involved with such employees to assist with proper documentation and follow-up.

- Ask that employees submit their self-evaluations to you before you write and present the formal evaluation.
- Schedule the time for the verbal review in advance so your employee can anticipate accommodating his or her schedule.

Even if your monthly or more frequent check-ins have been in a group or small group setting, the formal annual evaluation should be one-on-one. Elements for a successful evaluation should include:

1. A private office or room without danger of others eavesdropping
2. A comfortable place to sit
3. A paper copy of the evaluation for the employee to keep
4. Information about any raise or promotion the employee may be receiving as a result of the evaluation, if applicable

Sample Narrative

Thank you for taking the time to meet with me. As we discussed, this meeting is to go over your annual evaluation. You've already submitted to me your self-evaluation, which I reviewed while I was writing your formal evaluation.

[One positive sentence to summarize the evaluation]

You've demonstrated impressive professional growth this year.

[List multiple achievements/accomplishments]

You showed up with a positive attitude, engaging with your team and readily tackling obstacles that came up. You were able to think critically about creative solutions and then organize and delegate as appropriate to ensure that all necessary items were actioned. You not only stayed up-to-date on your required training, but you went above and beyond to earn two additional certificates and attend three extra education seminars here on campus.

[If there are items that have room for improvement, present them sandwiched between positive feedback]

When managing two or three projects at a time, you showed an impressive ability to multitask. However, when your workload increased to four projects, I did notice you become a little overwhelmed, which is understandable considering the attention to detail that you bring to every project. I think, over the next year, if you find yourself juggling multiple projects like that, delegating appropriate tasks to the ancillary team members may be an effective way to help you stay focused on the most important tasks and help you continue to deliver the quality product that you have been.

[Summarize the overall evaluation in different words than

the introduction]

Overall, myself and the other members of management were impressed with your dedication to expanding your knowledge base this year.

[Present decision to promote or increase pay]

Your achievements are on par with the job responsibilities required for a Level II technician, so it is my recommendation that you receive the promotion. The corresponding pay increase is eight percent more than your current salary. The new pay rate should take effect on the first day of your next pay period.

[Offer a token of appreciation for hard work in your own words]

Our team wouldn't have accomplished all that we were able to do over the past year without your help. Thank you for showing up and putting the work in. I am looking forward to working with you this coming year.

Made in the USA
Columbia, SC
27 March 2023

14346042R00028